AF131436

BOOK ANALYSIS

By Jessica Wheeler

The
Ambassadors
BY HENRY JAMES

HENRY JAMES 9

THE AMBASSADORS 13

SUMMARY 17

CHARACTER STUDY 23

Lambert Strether
Maria Gostrey
Waymarsh
Mrs Newsome

ANALYSIS 29

Success, privilege and superiority
The charm of Europe
Age and regret
Loyalty and obligation

FURTHER REFLECTION 37

FURTHER READING 41

HENRY JAMES

AMERICAN AUTHOR

- **Born in New York in 1843.**
- **Died in London in 1916.**
- **Notable works:**
  - *The Portrait of a Lady* (1881), novel
  - *The Turn of the Screw* (1898), novella
  - *The Golden Bowl* (1904), novel

Henry James was born in New York to wealthy parents Mary Walsh and Henry James Sr. He was one of five children, including the well-known psychologist William James. Henry James Sr. was an intellectual – a philosopher and a lecturer. Owing to this, he pursued many projects that took him and his family all over Europe; consequently, much of the James children's education was received through tutors rather than in schools. The family spent much time in France, where James became fluent in the language.

James briefly attended Harvard Law School, eventually choosing to pursue his passionate interest in literature instead. He continued to travel between London, America and France and wrote various pieces over the years which ranged from short stories and novels to reviews and other non-fiction works. James became a British citizen in 1915, a year before his death. He never married or had any children.

THE AMBASSADORS

A WITTY EXAMINATION OF WHAT IT MEANS TO REALLY LIVE

- **Genre:** novel
- **Reference edition:** James, H. (2018) *The Ambassadors*. London: Arcturus Publishing Ltd.
- **1st edition:** 1903
- **Themes:** duty, family, living life to the full, home and travel

The Ambassadors was originally published in serial form in the *North American Review* and then later the same year in novel form. There were many revisions and edits between publications, which has resulted in variations between editions. Nevertheless, James considered it to be his best novel.

This novel was written in the latter period of James' writing career, which many believe to be his most significant. He was increasingly influenced by the European writers he both studied and befriended, in particular the French realist Honoré de Balzac (1799-1850), on whom James lectured in America around the time of publication of *The Ambassadors.*

The novel is narrated in the third person, but follows the perspective of the protagonist Lambert Strether. The text is a somewhat comedic study of society, particularly its expectations and demands on the individual and of how life must be lived.

SUMMARY

The story opens with Strether's arrival at a hotel in England. He has travelled from America and has plans to meet his friend Waymarsh. Before Waymarsh arrives, Strether makes the acquaintance of Maria Gostrey, a fellow American whom he recognises from the journey to England. Maria claims to know Waymarsh, although not on intimate terms, and she explains to Strether that she has lived in Europe for many years and now acts as something of a tourist guide when she encounters English-speaking travellers. It is for this reason that she offers to show Strether around the town, and as a result they strike up a friendship.

Waymarsh then arrives at the hotel and Strether succeeds in enlisting his help in the task that has brought him from America to Europe. Strether and Waymarsh are to make their way to London, and Maria decides to accompany them and act as their guide. Maria and Strether go to the theatre together, and he explains to her what he is doing in Europe: at the request of his employer and potential future wife, Mrs Newsome, he is travelling to Paris in search of her son Chad. Strether is tasked with bringing Chad Newsome back to America as his family fear he has fallen in with a bad crowd and is throwing his life and money away in Paris. Mrs Newsome wants her son to come home to take over the family business. Maria guesses that Strether's successful and profitable marriage to Mrs Newsome depends on his carrying out her wishes with regard to her son.

Strether and Waymarsh arrive in Paris and Strether makes a visit to the address that he has for Chad. It turns out that Chad is not there, but has made a trip to Cannes, and his friend John Bilham is looking after his flat. Bilham invites Strether for breakfast the following morning. Strether likes Bilham despite himself, and when Maria arrives in Paris he seeks her opinion on the situation. Maria says that she will meet Bilham herself, and hopefully Chad, and she will be able to figure out what is what. Maria, Strether and Waymarsh attend the theatre and extend an invite to Bilham; however, Chad shows up in his place.

Strether explains to Chad that he has come to bring him home, but he is surprised to find that Chad has matured into quite the gentleman, contrary to the belief held by the family back in America, who fear he has been ruined by Parisian culture. Strether spends some days with Chad in Paris and tries to ascertain whether or not there is a woman in his life. He feels increasingly that Chad is keeping something from him.

It emerges that Chad has some connection to a countess by the name of Madame de Vionette and her daughter Jeanne. Strether meets both women, and it becomes clear that Madame de Vionette is responsible for the positive changes that are evident in Chad, although the exact nature of their relationship is not yet obvious. Strether begins to feel that Mrs Newsome may be wrong about bringing her son home from Paris, and this in turn causes Strether to question his own situation and the way he has lived his life so far. Maria leaves Paris to visit a sick friend and Strether spends some more time with Madame de Vionette.

Due to Strether's failure to bring Chad home, Sarah Pocock, Chad's sister, arrives in Paris to find out what is going on. When Strether and Sarah eventually sit down together to converse, it is apparent that they do not see eye to eye and that Sarah is disappointed in Strether for letting her mother down. Sarah and her husband and sister-in-law are getting ready to leave Paris to return to America (stopping in Switzerland on the way), and Waymarsh informs Strether that he will be leaving with them.

Strether takes a trip out of the city to clear his head, but while he is out for a walk he sees Chad and Madame de Vionette taking a boat trip together and realises the nature that their relationship has secretly taken all along – they are lovers. This realisation devastates Strether, as he feels like he has been a fool and the Newsomes have been right to think that Chad has got himself into a compromising situation whilst in Paris. As a result of his disenchantment with Paris, Strether decides that he will return home to America, despite the fact this his prospects of a relationship with Mrs Newsome are ruined.

In their last meeting, Strether advises Chad against going back to America. Instead he urges him to be loyal to Madame de Vionette and not succumb to the pressure of his overbearing relations. Chad goes against this advice and decides that he will return home to inherit the family business and the fortune that comes with it. Maria reveals her true affections for Strether when she asks him to stay with her in Paris, but he turns her down due to his sense of disappointment in his experience of Europe and the way it has fooled him.

CHARACTER STUDY

LAMBERT STRETHER

Strether is the protagonist of the story. He is a man in his mid-50s who sees himself as something of a failure, especially compared with his friend Waymarsh. He tells Maria that he has not been as successful in making money as Waymarsh has, and he seems to carry a lot of regrets about his life and the way he has lived it. The reader learns that Strether had a wife and child, and that he married young. He lost his wife and, soon after, his little boy. He is hard on himself with regard to the death of his son, as he believes that if he had not been so lost in grief over his wife, he would have been able to do more to save his son.

Strether is an anxious person who second-guesses and criticises himself constantly. He tells Maria Gostrey in the first chapters of the novel that he has difficulty living in the present, and she subsequently diagnoses him with an inability to enjoy life. Strether lives his life according to the wishes of others and the dictates of the society to which he belongs. Spending time in Paris, and seeing the changes that have taken place in Chad Newsome after his time spent there, alter Strether's view of how life should be lived.

MARIA GOSTREY

Maria acts as a confidante and friend to Strether throughout the novel, beginning very soon after they meet each other. She is experienced and knowledgeable when it comes to European culture, and she displays a sense of independence and self-confidence which contrasts greatly with Strether's perpetual habit of doubting himself. She is the vessel for Strether's development in the novel, as she is the person who he constantly turns to for advice and to discuss his thoughts and feelings.

Maria does not care what others think of her, yet she conducts herself with class and dignity. She has the ability to figure people out very quickly, which is something that she prides herself on. She appears to be more of an observer in the novel than a participant in the drama, even taking herself out of Paris for a time in order to avoid being dragged into the situation with Strether, Chad and Madame de Vionette.

In the end, it is clear that Maria is in love with Strether, but due to his newfound independence and strength of character he chooses not to stay with her in Paris and instead to go home and face the mistakes he feels he has made in an attempt to salvage a happier and more fulfilling life for himself.

WAYMARSH

Waymarsh is a lawyer and a friend of Strether's. Like Strether, he too is American. Waymarsh claims early on in the novel that he does not like Europe and its customs as much as he does those of his homeland. He differs in temperament to his friend Strether – he is more serious and critical of the world around him. Waymarsh's temperament could be affected by his strained relationship with his wife: the couple are separated, but not divorced, and she makes it her business to regularly write abusive letters to him, whilst conducting herself in a manner which brings much shame to the morally rigid lawyer. Waymarsh is unaffected by the beauties and charms of Parisian culture that leave such an impression on Strether, and he disapproves of the changes that he witnesses in his friend over the course of their stay. When Sarah Pocock arrives in Paris, it seems that Waymarsh may have feelings for her. The two characters are similar in their rigid morality and sense of superiority.

MRS NEWSOME

Mrs Newsome is present as a force throughout the novel, although her character never actually materially takes part in the story. She is a wealthy widow and potentially the future wife of Lambert Strether. It is clear throughout the story that their relationship is not based on love, but that Strether admires Mrs Newsome as she is a virtuous and honourable woman.

Mrs Newsome, although an absent character, drives much of the plot of *The Ambassadors,* as it is upon her request that Strether travels to Paris in search of her son, and it is in line with her wishes and expectations that he tries and/ or fails to conduct himself and form his judgements. Mrs Newsome exerts a massive amount of control over Strether's character, but also over the lives of her children Sarah Pocock and Chad Newsome. She is representative of the American matriarch in the 1900s.

ANALYSIS

SUCCESS, PRIVILEGE AND SUPERIORITY

Strether compares himself to his friend Waymarsh and feels that he is inferior to him because of Waymarsh's success. It is clear, though, that Strether measures this success on the basis of Waymarsh's financial circumstances and his ability to make more money than Strether himself ever has. In his assessment of Waymarsh's superiority, he does not consider the relationship that the lawyer has with his wife, or Waymarsh's seeming inability to find any joy in life.

Another count upon which characters seem to judge those around them in this novel is that of morality or virtue. The Newsomes are determined to bring Chad home from Paris as they fear that he has fallen in with a bad crowd. They see the artist types found in Europe as essentially idle and morally corrupt. This perception is not changed when Sarah Pocock arrives in Paris and comes face to face with Madame de Vionette – a woman of fortune and status, like Sarah's mother, but whom Sarah sees as inferior due to her lack of virtue. With the knowledge that Madame has been the facilitator of Chad's transformation into a gentleman, his sister judges that this transformation is not for the better. In this way, despite the fact that Madame de Vionette is as financially privileged as Mrs Newsome, Sarah Pocock judges that she is lesser in terms of honourability.

The novel deals mostly with characters that come from a more privileged class, and the narrative examines how the members of this stratum of society view each other and judge the social hierarchy in which they operate. The Newsomes consider themselves to be at the top of the scale based on their superior morality as well as their financial privilege.

THE CHARM OF EUROPE

Chad's family send Strether to Paris to bring him home as they are worried that the novelty and romance of life abroad has captivated their son and brother and caused him to give up his respectability. They feel threatened by that which is unknown and unfamiliar to them, for they feel that it has the power to enchant and lead one astray. This sentiment has some truth to it, as is later shown when Strether and eventually Jim Pocock travel to Paris and are taken in by the new sights and foreign culture.

Maria Gostrey, as a self-proclaimed and self-appointed guide to the American tourists who endeavour to explore the charms of Europe, says that her purpose in this role is to help the travellers fill their desire for enchantment and send them home as quickly as possible.

Strether feels that when he is in Europe, and away from the dreary constraints of his life in America, he can enjoy life so much more and not feel the need to pass negative judgement on all he encounters as his friend Waymarsh is accustomed to doing. Strether feels freer and less inhibited as it seems to him that Parisian society is not as rigid and socially prescriptive as that which he is used to in America. However, by the end of the novel it seems to Strether that he has been a fool to believe this and to be taken in by the charming novelty of a new country. He sees that he has been deceived by the people around him due to the fact that he was rendered gullible and unsuspecting by the romantic impression of Parisian culture that he opened himself up to.

AGE AND REGRET

Throughout the novel, Strether exhibits a sense of regret and feelings of failure, which are connected to his acknowledgement that he is no longer in the comfort of his youth. This creates a strong theme within the story. Strether compares himself to his friend Waymarsh, who is of a similar age, and he decides that he has wasted his years trying to achieve and always coming short. When Strether reaches Paris, he really starts to ponder on this as he looks at those around him who seem to be living life to its full potential. He advises Bilham not to waste his youth as he himself has done, and he tries to encourage Chad not to return home to America as it would be a choice made under the pressure of his family's desires and the dictates of society.

Even after Strether admits to Maria that he suffers from a failure to appreciate life as he finds it difficult to keep his mind in the present, he spends much of the novel wrapped up in his own thoughts of how he should have lived his life differently. He thinks back to when he was young and newly married and how the loss of his wife to illness affected him so deeply. He believes that his failure to deal with this loss also cost him the life of his child. He blames himself although there was nothing he could have done, and nothing he can do in the present, and continues to spend his time submerged and consumed by his regrets.

LOYALTY AND OBLIGATION

As Strether is in Europe at the request of Mrs Newsome to carry out a mission assigned by her, he feels obligated to conduct himself according to her expectations. For this reason, Strether feels that he is betraying her when he gets to Paris and he begins to understand why Chad may have chosen to stay there for the length of time that he has. He begins to hold back details in his letters, and feels that he himself is being deceptive, for he does not want to admit to Mrs Newsome that he has been impressed by Parisian culture. Strether struggles throughout the story with the loyalty that he feels towards

Mrs Newsome and the need to maintain the attitude of condemnation of European culture that he left America, and Mrs Newsome, with.

When Sarah Pocock arrives in Paris, she is disappointed in Strether as she feels that he has failed in his obligations to her mother and her family. Furthermore, Sarah feels that Chad should want to go back to America and be with his family out of a sense of loyalty to them. The sense of duty is very straightforward for Sarah. She is not moved by the novelty and romance of Paris or its artistic wonders, for she is held firm in the purpose that has brought her there – to remind her brother of his obligations to his kin.

By the end of the novel, Strether has changed his perspective and now advises Chad that he is indebted to Madame de Vionette for the seeming improvements that she has brought about in him, and that he has a duty towards her on account of the romantic feelings they have nurtured for each other. Strether's last request of Chad is that he remain loyal to Madame de Vionette, although he does not elaborate on what he means by this.

In this way, many of the character's actions are born out of a sense of commitment to others. This fulfilment of duty is what gives the Newsomes a sense of honour and superiority. When it becomes apparent that Strether has failed in his loyalty to Mrs Newsome and her wishes, his prospect of a future with her is lost.

FURTHER REFLECTION

SOME QUESTIONS TO THINK ABOUT...

- Discuss James' writing style in this novel. Compare it to his writing style in one of his short stories.
- Discuss the relationship between Strether and Maria Gostrey. Are there romantic feelings between these two characters?
- The novel is split into 12 'books'. What effect do you think this structure has on the novel?
- Madame de Vionette seems to purposely get Strether in trouble with Sarah Pocock. Why do you think she does this?
- Why do you think Chad Newsome decides to return home to America at the end of the novel?
- Why do you think the author has chosen to keep it a secret from the reader what item Mr Newsome invented that resulted in the family's successful business?

- Mrs Newsome is an absent yet forceful presence in the novel. Discuss the effect that her character's physical absence from the action has on the other characters.
- Why do you think Henry James decided to call this novel *The Ambassadors*? Would you give the text a different title?

We want to hear from you!
Leave a comment on your online library
and share your favourite books on social media!

FURTHER READING

REFERENCE EDITION

- James, H. (2018) *The Ambassadors*. London: Arcturus Publishing Ltd.

MORE FROM BRIGHTSUMMARIES.COM

- Reading guide – *The Portrait of a Lady* by Henry James.
- Reading guide – *The Turn of the Screw* by Henry James.
- Reading guide – *What Maisie Knew* by Henry James.

www.brightsummaries.com

Ebook EAN: 9782808017503

Paperback EAN: 9782808017510

Legal Deposit: D/2019/12603/42

Cover: © Primento

Digital conception by Primento, the digital partner of
publishers.